D0845693

TROPE

ICONIC COMPOSERS

A Celebration of Music's Extraordinary Composers

Illustrated by

DAVID LEE CSICSKO

Text by

**NICHOLAS CSICSKO
& EMI FERGUSON**

CONTENTS

JAMIE
BERNSTEIN

Internationally acclaimed writer, broadcaster, and filmmaker

What a perfectly magical thing music is. Music has the power to light up our emotions, making us feel joyous, sad, wistful, or madly excited—or even make us feel emotions we don't have words to describe. My father, Leonard Bernstein, is one of the many gifted composers mentioned in this delightful book. He was also a teacher who loved to share music with others—especially young people. He said music can "name the unnameable and communicate the unknowable." That's a big part of music's magic: it begins to cast its strongest spell at the precise point where words stop working.

One of the most extraordinary engines of Western music has been the symphony orchestra. For centuries, this large group of players produced a multiplicity of sounds—and sheer volume—that could not be found elsewhere. Can you imagine how thrilling it must have been in the early 1800s to hear something as purely LOUD as Ludwig van Beethoven's *Ninth Symphony*, with full orchestra, soloists, and chorus?! Alas, Beethoven was the one person who could not be amazed by that phenomenon, as by then, he had become profoundly deaf when he wrote his glorious *Ninth*. And yet, somehow, he could hear the symphony in his head, and wrote down those thousands of notes so they could be performed for us.

Throughout history, many superb composers who happened to be women, or people of color, were unfairly overlooked. This book is part of the current, ongoing repair of those omissions by including composers that ought to be familiar to us—and with any luck, will become so. These gifted artists are finally getting the attention they deserve.

Dedicating one's life to music has never been the most recommended path to wealth. Many of the composers in this book worked other jobs to keep themselves afloat. Hildegard von Bingen got around this problem by being an abbess in a convent in 12th century Germany. Within those protected walls, Hildegard produced astonishing works of music, philosophy, and medical science.

In early 18th century Germany, Johann Sebastian Bach kept his family fed by writing church music that would be performed every Sunday. By the end of that century, the Austrian composer Joseph Haydn was the palace musician for the Esterházy noble family. Haydn really lucked out with this job because his patrons were such music fans that they provided him with an entire orchestra. This is sort of like a rich person supporting a gifted baseball pitcher by providing him with an entire team!

Another famous Austrian composer, Wolfgang Amadeus Mozart, was not so lucky. Although he took every job that came his way, he was always broke. The story goes that he and his beloved wife, Constanze, would dance around the living room to warm themselves up because they didn't have enough money to buy wood for the stove. When we listen to Mozart's heavenly music, we feel sorrowful for how much he suffered because he wasn't treasured in his own lifetime.

In the 1900s, composers found new ways to make a living beyond concert halls and theaters. Movies and television need lots of music! My own dad, Leonard Bernstein, wrote the score for the Oscar-winning film *On the Waterfront* in 1954. Today, video games are a rich, new environment for composers like Nobuo Uematsu.

Leonard Bernstein was curious about every kind of music: Balinese gamelan, Japanese koto, Arabic oud, Indian sitar—he embraced it all. He understood that music could be magnificent no matter where it came from. He wanted the power of music to reach everyone, everywhere. For him, music was the essence of communication. He loved to share music. Sharing meant teaching; teaching meant reaching; and reaching meant connecting. He truly believed that music could help human beings rise above their differences and become a peaceful, united, mutually nurturing entity. Music is humanity at its best—and this book will introduce you to some of its finest heroes.

LaROB K. RAFAEL

Classical music DJ, artist, and activist

When we look at the world around us, one thing is clear—everyone has a story! Each person we encounter could tell us something unique about their experience on this planet and we would walk away richer than before.

In classical music though, we have been trained to appreciate just a few stories. We are taught to believe that Ludwig van Beethoven's achievements against all odds, Wolfgang Amadeus Mozart's young genius, or Johann Sebastian Bach's unending catalog and work ethic are the most significant stories to be told. They *are* significant and important to contextualize classical music in the 21st century. But they are not the only important stories.

As we remember that everyone has a story, we must begin to incorporate the stories of those who for far too long have been overlooked—composers whose lives and features look a little different than Beethoven and Bach.

The beauty of music is that it can transport you through melody and empathy into a new world, allowing you to connect with someone you might not have otherwise known. Hearing the music of Florence Price, a Black female composer of the early 1900s, gives you a little insight into her journey. Learning about the life of Joseph Bologne, Chevalier de Saint-Georges, a fencer and leader of a battalion in the French Revolution, gives you context for his music.

It wasn't until after college that I was introduced to the history of Harry T. Burleigh, a Black composer who was crucial to developing a true American classical sound, and someone who is featured in this book. He made traditional Spirituals available to classically trained artists by arranging them in a classical form. Suddenly, I was able to perform the music I had grown up listening to in church for classical audiences. I was able to tell my own story instead of only interpreting others because I had found a composer that looked like me and shared my experiences.

There are so many female composers and composers of color who deserve the same recognition we give Johannes Brahms and Franz Schubert. Highlighting them does not take away from the greatness of Brahms; instead, it creates a fuller picture of our musical landscape, not just a sliver of musical history and greatness. When we showcase the contributions of Black, Indigenous, Latin, Asian, and African composers, we present a story grounded in truth and begin to create equity in the arts!

There are so many fantastic composers and this book is a great way for you to expand both your knowledge and your classical music playlist. From the early music of Hildegard von Bingen to the video game music of Nobuo Uematsu—you'd be surprised at the significance of these composers to musical history overall!

Music nourishes the soul and is ever changing. *Iconic Composers* highlights the lives of 50 people who made glorious music. While some are already famous, Nicholas Csicsko, Emi Ferguson, and I strove to equally shine a spotlight on many composers we need to know.

I've always been on a classical music adventure, and my friends have been my guides. A special thank you to David Syrek, Lawrence Rapchak, Tom Bachtell, Ann Murray, Michelle Areyzaga, Peter McDowell, Christopher Bell, Youming Chen, Michael Murphy, Carol Falcone Chiantis, Gary Alexander, John Cipriano, Mark Larsen, Jennifer Nelson, Roberta Allen, Carol Nichols Loehrke, and my composer friends Nigel Hess, Stacy Garrop, John McDowell, George N. Gianopoulos, and Brandon Harrington. Also, a giant thank-you to Jamie Bernstein and LaRob K. Rafael for their contributions to the book.

And in celebration of my music heroes: pianist Dame Myra Hess, who gave 1,698 concerts in London during World War II and Nicholas Falcone, an Italian immigrant who broke the color barrier and desegregated the band at the University of Michigan in the 1930s. Your selflessness continues to inspire.

DAVID LEE CSICSKO

It feels impossible to reduce 1000+ years of musical creators and innovators to a list of only 50. Through this book, our hope is that readers will be able to see the vast expanses of classical music—a genre that encompasses SO many kinds of music and people who continue to inspire us all to revel in the silences, and make some noise!

Our special thanks to our family, friends, and colleagues who lent their expertise and eagle eyes. Most especially to Jeff Gatto.

This is the list that we wish we could have had as kids. But, there are SO MANY MORE composers who are not in this book. Never stop discovering new voices and listening to their music.

NICHOLAS CSICSKO & EMI FERGUSON

ICONIC
COMPOSERS

HILDEGARD
VON BINGEN

The 12th century power nun

Many have wondered who the authors of the countless "anonymous" works throughout history were. Were they like me? Why didn't or why couldn't they take authorship of their works—works that inspire and uplift us. In 1929, American writer Virginia Woolf proclaimed that for most of history, "anonymous" was a woman. We see so few female composers in our history pages and are only now seeing a greater representation of marginalized voices in classical music as a whole. One early outlier is Hildegard von Bingen.

Hard to categorize, Hildegard was a feminist, mystic, physician, artist, writer, biologist, linguist, religious leader, poet, and composer. Living to 80 years old, she took advantage of every hour she was given. Entering a convent at the age of eight, Hildegard received an education unlike many women of her day. Wanting other women to have the same educational opportunity, she established her own religious community for women where she studied and wrote about theology, arts, sciences, and humanities. She wrote music that her fellow nuns performed in the service of daily church-life that contained a degree of freedom and imagination that was unusual for her time. Hildegard's strong sense of individuality helped her to develop a unique compositional voice that sprung from her heart. She even wrote a church musical for her fellow nuns to perform called *Order of the Virtues*.

Hildegard fought her entire life to create a community that enabled women to pursue the same academic and artistic interests and receive the same respect as their male counterparts. In a time where women's thoughts and opinions were often disregarded, Hildegard was so respected that in 1148, the Pope recognized her life-long mystical visions as legitimate revelations from God. Almost 1000 years later, Pope Benedict XVI bestowed one of the highest honors of the Catholic Church, making her a Saint and Doctor of the Church.

HILDEGARD

HILDEGARD VON BINGEN

1098 – 1179

BERMERSHEIM VOR DER HÖHE (GERMANY)

GUILLAUME
DE MACHAUT

The survivor who took the Mass to new heights

No one expected a kid from small-town France to become known throughout Europe as a highly influential poet and composer, and so no one recorded the details of Guillaume de Machaut's family or early years. The first thing we know about Guillaume is that he left home at the age of 23, getting his big break traveling Europe as part of the entourage of the King of Bohemia. He served the King as his secretary for 13 years while also creating poetry and music that pushed boundaries. Like every iconic songwriter, Guillaume wrote about love, influencing other writers including Geoffrey Chaucer and Christine de Pizan. Musically, he helped to establish a completely new style of composition, the Ars Nova.

Guillaume's most famous work today is his *Messe de Nostre Dame* which was revolutionary as the first complete mass by one composer. This meant that the church service had one unifying vision rather than many different composers contributing music without consideration for the overall flow. Having a unified vision motivated composers to imagine writing larger and more creative works that allowed their personalities to shine through and individual styles to develop. This increased personalization essentially created the modern definition of a composer. Though many remember Guillaume for his groundbreaking church music, he also wrote hundreds of secular pieces of music, often about courtly love, that secured his renown.

Guillaume was fortunate to survive the Black Death that took the lives of almost half of Europe's population from 1346-1352. In his 70s, he collected his life's work and compiled and preserved his compositions himself for future generations to enjoy.

GUILLAUME DE MACHAUT

1300 – 1377

REIMS (FRANCE)

CLAUDIO MONTEVERDI

The rule breaking father of opera

Born into a musical family, Claudio Monteverdi divided his career working for both the court and the church. After serving the Mantuan court for over 20 years, Claudio took leadership of music at St. Mark's Cathedral in Venice where he spent the rest of his life. It was the height of the Italian Renaissance and Claudio rubbed shoulders and discussed ideas with pioneering Renaissance figures including astronomer Galileo Galilei and artist Peter Paul Rubens.

Like Ludwig van Beethoven, Igor Stravinsky, Elvis Presley, Jimi Hendrix, and all other musicians who push musical boundaries, Claudio battled critics who wanted his music silenced. Although Claudio faced criticism in the press for his use of dissonance, combinations of notes that were unusual at the time, his patrons and the public loved the raw emotions his musical choices conjured.

In 1607, audiences heard Claudio's first opera, *Orfeo*. The opera contained vivid imagery that illustrated the story so compellingly that it forever changed what musical storytelling could be. His use of harmony, instrumentation, and contrast struck the hearts and minds of his supporters, and his operas were so inspiring he became known as the father of opera. Audiences became enamored with opera as a result, creating a demand that inspired the first public opera house to open with enormous fanfare.

After war and plague ravaged much of Italy in 1630, a devastated and tired Claudio stepped away from composing to become a priest and focus on his spirituality. Claudio eventually returned to public life, composing some of his greatest works in his last decade. When he died at the age of 76, Claudio was well respected and his musical style was embraced by composers who continued to build on his foundation.

MONTEVERDI

CLAUDIO MONTEVERDI

1567 – 1643

CREMONA (ITALY)

BARBARA
STROZZI

The muse of Venice

Barbara Strozzi ruffled quite a few feathers when she became the most published composer of her lifetime. Celebrated far and wide for her masterful performances singing and playing the lute, she achieved success while raising four children as a single mother, fighting to have her voice heard in a society and culture where women's voices were marginalized.

As the daughter of one of Venice's most renowned poets and opera librettists, Barbara grew up immersed in the city's vibrant artistic scene. She mingled and learned from academics, cultural leaders, and composers who would come to the Strozzi household for meetings of Venice's elite musical society. It was there that Barbara performed to such acclaim that she was heralded as one of Venice's finest musicians by the time she was only 15 years old.

Barbara was often the only woman in the room for these intimate performances. She created every aspect of the performance, playing music she composed while singing lyrics she wrote. As a woman succeeding in a field dominated by men, she faced slander from those who sought to defame her character. At the age of 25 she published her first volume of music in which she penned a special note expressing her concerns about the expected slander, simply because she was a woman. Despite this, Barbara succeeded where so many women did not, and could not, weaving references to gender inequality into her music. It would have been no easy feat for her to publish just one composition under her own name, but Barbara published eight books of compositions, fighting and conquering societal barriers every step of the way.

BARBARA STROZZI

1619 – 1677

VENICE (ITALY)

JACQUET de La GUERRE

ÉLISABETH JACQUET DE LA GUERRE

1665 – 1729

PARIS (FRANCE)

ÉLISABETH
JACQUET DE LA GUERRE

The star of the Sun King's court

Élisabeth Jacquet de La Guerre was born into a long line of wealthy musicians and harpsichord builders. She was first recognized at only five years old when her virtuosity at the keyboard earned her the nickname "la petite merveille", the small wonder, at the court of Louis XIV.

In late 17th century France, there was only one place to be as a composer: the court of Louis XIV, the Sun King. He brought together the best musicians, poets, painters, writers, architects, sculptors, and playwrights of the day to experiment and create some of the French Baroque's most magnificent works of art. If you could make it there, you could make it anywhere. After her celebrated performances as a child, a teenaged Élisabeth became a regular part of Louis XIV's court, rubbing shoulders with France's most influential composers including the founding father of French Baroque opera, Jean-Baptiste Lully, one of Louis XIV's partners in making the French court a cradle of creativity.

Élisabeth was the first French woman to have an opera produced in France and was a pioneer in bringing the Italian sonata form into the French musical style. Élisabeth's first published collection of compositions for the harpsichord was groundbreaking because it was unusual to write for the solo keyboard in her lifetime. A master performer and improviser at the harpsichord, she helped build the foundation of repertoire for the instrument. It was uncommon for women to continue to make music publicly once they married, but Élisabeth married a musician who encouraged and defended her work as a performer and composer. Her works continue to inspire performers today for their ingenuity, virtuosity, and perspective.

ANTONIO VIVALDI

The unexpected feminist who gave wings to the Baroque concerto

"The Red Priest" is a fitting nickname for a man with shockingly red hair who began studying to become a priest at the age of 15. However, when it turned out that the priesthood was not for Antonio Vivaldi, fate gave him a different path, and he became a highly influential composer, violinist, and teacher in an unusual way.

Antonio ended up working at one of the most unique orphanages in Venice, the Ospedale della Pietà that housed and supported orphaned girls. Here, he was a part of something truly amazing, transforming the orphanage into one of the most popular concert venues of the day. Antonio trained young female orphans on musical instruments and wrote much of his music, specifically concertos, to showcase their incredible talents. This was quite unusual at the time as women were often prohibited from playing and performing at all, making Antonio somewhat of an unexpected feminist!

People came from far and wide to hear Antonio's music which became well known during his lifetime. Even Johann Sebastian Bach was a fan, rearranging several of Antonio's concertos for performances of his own. Antonio eventually left the orphanage to pursue greater fame, writing many operas and oratorios and even being knighted by the King of Austria. Today, Antonio's music is played worldwide, with his collection of violin concertos, *The Four Seasons*, being amongst the most popular pieces of classical music repertoire taking listeners through the four seasons of the year with fantastical representations of nature through sound.

VIVALDI

ANTONIO VIVALDI

1678 – 1741

VENICE (ITALY)

HANDEL

GEORGE FRIDERIC HANDEL

1685 – 1759

HALLE (GERMANY)

GEORGE FRIDERIC HANDEL

England's greatest German composer, Hallelujah!

At the age of 19, George Frideric Handel claimed that his music saved his life. George found himself in a sword duel with a musical rival who struck what would have been a critical blow but was saved by his own opera manuscript in his jacket pocket that stopped the sword. George thereafter believed music was his destiny. His parents did not always feel the same way, initially forbidding him from studying music. George would sneak away and find a keyboard with which to experiment. His parents soon realized the only path forward was to support the talent and interest of their unrelenting son.

Born the same year as Johann Sebastian Bach, the two would become known for establishing much of Baroque musical style. Although born in German-speaking lands, George traveled throughout Europe picking up musical styles as he went. He spent part of his youth in Italy, and eventually settled in London where he often served royalty and became one of England's greatest composers. His English oratorio *Messiah* was his most popular work in his time and has become his most recognized piece today. The "Hallelujah Chorus" from the *Messiah* is one of the most performed pieces of classical music in all of history and remains a staple for many during the holiday season. The *Messiah* not only impacted English choral music but also influenced composers of future generations and differing styles. After hearing the *Messiah*, Joseph Haydn exclaimed, "This man is the master of us all!" Ludwig van Beethoven felt similarly, remarking, "Handel is the greatest composer who ever lived. I would bare my head and kneel at his grave." George eventually became a British citizen and his music has been performed at the coronation of every British monarch from his lifetime to today. He is buried in the poets corner of Westminster Abbey amongst the greatest English legends, including William Shakespeare and Charles Dickens.

JOHANN SEBASTIAN BACH

The king of counterpoint

Johann Sebastian Bach was just one member of a long line of musicians; in fact, he was not the most famous Bach until long after his death. Johann's parents, grandparents, and great-grandparents were all musicians and he passed down the family trade to his own children who became famous composers in their own right. Johann had so many kids (20!) he could have started a small orchestra with them alone. There are wonderful stories of the Bach family singing, playing, and creating music together that have lasted for centuries. Johann viewed music as the family profession, and he worked to improve every day. He was able to write with incredible speed as well as improvise to a legendary level with stories of musical duels and competitions in which he always triumphed.

Johann didn't travel far in his life. With so many kids at home and an exhausting job composing music and teaching students at Leipzig's famous St. Thomas Church, he was extraordinarily busy. Yet, he found time to compose for fun in addition to writing the music he had to create for church services each week. On days off, you could find Johann down the street at Zimmerman's Coffee House with local students, musicians, and friends, drinking beer and coffee and playing music into the night.

Although much of his music was neglected in the decades after his death, composers throughout history and today have found inspiration in the craftsmanship and poignancy with which all his music is imbued. Johann's music is so universal that it speaks to artists and audiences of all kinds throughout the world today who are constantly reinventing and reimagining it in their own image.

BACH

JOHANN SEBASTIAN BACH

1685 – 1750

EISENACH (GERMANY)

SANCHO

IGNATIUS SANCHO

1729 – 1780

SLAVE SHIP IN THE ATLANTIC OCEAN

IGNATIUS SANCHO

*The composer who helped bring
abolition to England*

Becoming a successful composer lies at the intersection of hard work and the right opportunities. Some people are given the opportunity, and others, like Ignatius Sancho, make it for themselves. Ignatius was brought to England as an enslaved child when he was two years old, going on to become the first person of African descent to vote in England. With the help of a household visitor, Ignatius taught himself to read and write as a child against his enslavers' wishes. He eventually escaped when he was 20 years old.

As a free person, Ignatius continued his musical and literary studies while also composing, acting, and writing. Over the next two decades, he would marry, have seven children, and open his own grocery store in London that became a well-known meeting place for many of London's literary and political writers and critics.

In his lifetime, he would self-publish a treatise on music theory and four volumes of compositions, mostly dance and social music, proudly emblazoning on the front covers "Composed by an African." By the time of his death, Ignatius was a celebrated figure for his writing on 18th century English life and politics as well as his active engagement in philosophy and debate. Ignatius's letters to various news outlets served as an 18th century social media feed, showcasing political, economic, and cultural concerns. His writing advocating for the abolition of the slave trade encouraged readers to judge the hearts of people, not their complexion. After his death, Ignatius's son published 160 of his letters in a collection titled *The Letters of the Late Ignatius Sancho, An African* which became a bestseller, reprinting four times before the turn of the 19th century, and inspiring generations to come.

JOSEPH HAYDN

*Father of the symphony
and mentor to future generations*

Joseph Haydn was a problem solver and an optimist from an early age. As a young boy, Joseph moved away from home to begin his musical career, but the family he lived with barely fed him. The starving Joseph soon figured out a solution to this problem, discovering that there was free food at the musical performances held in the homes of the aristocracy. Joseph quickly worked to make sure he was invited to perform at as many aristocratic homes as possible, turning these concerts into both his musical classroom and his pantry. His knack for problem solving stayed with him his whole life. Rather than being a shooting star, his musical development was slow and steady, resulting in mastery and fame over a long career.

After working his way up the musical ladder, Joseph found employment with the wealthy Esterházy family where he enjoyed an illustrious career writing many symphonies and string quartets. By the time Joseph left the Esterházy's at age 58, he was one of the most famous and sought-after composers in Europe. He left the Esterházy court to travel to London where he was overwhelmed by praise and honors for his compositions. He was even given an honorary doctorate from the University of Oxford, a title he would add to his signature for the remainder of his life. Joseph returned to Vienna where he produced some of his greatest late works—pieces that show his humor, imagination, and his ability to represent the physical world through sound.

Joseph mentored the next generation of composers including Wolfgang Amadeus Mozart and Ludwig van Beethoven. Joseph and Mozart played in a string quartet together, building a high level of mutual respect, and influenced each other's compositions. Joseph's hard work, kindness, and humility stayed with him his whole life, inspiring both those around him and generations to come.

JOSEPH HAYDN

1732 – 1809

ROHRAU (AUSTRIA)

JOSEPH BOLOGNE

*The best swordsman in France who tickled
Marie Antoinette's ears and threw Joseph Haydn a bone*

Joseph Bologne was one of those people who excelled at everything he did. He was an incredible musician, athlete, dancer, and military leader, as well as being ravishingly handsome. He was born in Guadeloupe, a French island in the Caribbean, to a plantation-owning French father and an enslaved Senegalese mother. At seven years old, Joseph's father took him to France to further his education, where he studied not only music, but also fencing. He became such a good fencer that by his early 20s, he became a bodyguard to the French King after having beaten all the best swordsmen in France, earning him the title "Chevalier".

He was not only the best swordsman in France, but also one of the most acclaimed musicians. Though he was considered the obvious choice to lead the Paris Opera, due to a racist smear campaign, he didn't get the job despite the support of many of the city's musicians, aristocrats, and even the Queen, Marie Antoinette, who was one of Joseph's biggest fans. As a man of mixed race, Joseph's life was heavily impacted by racist laws that prevented him from inheriting his father's aristocratic titles, marrying someone of his societal stature, and having the opportunities, respect, and privileges afforded his white peers. Even with these barriers, Joseph founded his own orchestra, regarded as one of the finest in France. He even commissioned Haydn's famous *Paris Symphonies* that premiered with Joseph conducting to great acclaim. In addition to championing music by other composers, Joseph wrote his own music, showcasing his virtuosic violin playing as well as ensemble pieces that were played all over Paris.

Joseph's later life was deeply affected by the French Revolution with its goals of equality and liberty for all. These ideals inspired Joseph to join the Revolutionary Army as a leader and the colonel of the first all-Black regiment in Europe that was nicknamed the Légion Saint-Georges for Joseph's leadership.

BOLOGNE

JOSEPH BOLOGNE, CHEVALIER DE SAINT-GEORGES

1745 – 1799

BAILLIF (GUADELOUPE)

WOLFGANG AMADEUS MOZART

The humor loving boy genius

By the age of 14, Wolfgang Amadeus Mozart had performed for many of the kings and queens of Europe, composed symphonies and operas, and was even knighted by the Pope. He was the model child prodigy, raised by the original stage parents. Much of Wolfgang's formative years were spent on the road, performing with his sister across the courts of Europe, leaving little time for him to lose his youthful humor which stayed with him throughout his life. This childlike demeanor can be found in his lifelong love for games, which he often weaved into his music, and in his letters which are filled with pet names for his family and friends.

As an adult, Wolfgang struggled to surpass the recognition he received in childhood. However, his music continued to evolve, leaving a collection of instrumental and opera works that helped to define the Classical period and inspire future generations of composers. Wolfgang wrote music to suit his and his patrons' purposes, sometimes a piano concerto to show off his skills at the keyboard, and other times an opera, the most popular medium of live entertainment at the time. Hanging out with royalty as a child gave Wolfgang a lifelong thirst for all things fancy, especially clothes, that stayed with him until his death. This taste for luxury, in addition to other distractions, led him to always be short on cash despite earning more than enough to support himself.

In his short 35 years, he wrote an immense amount of music and was known for working incredibly long hours, churning out masterpiece after masterpiece. A combination of overwork, poor health, and bad luck led to Wolfgang's early death but not before he composed over 600 works including symphonies, concertos, chamber music, operas, and so much more!

WOLFGANG AMADEUS MOZART

1756 – 1791

SALZBURG (AUSTRIA)

BEETHOVEN

LUDWIG VAN BEETHOVEN

1770 – 1827

BONN (GERMANY)

LUDWIG VAN BEETHOVEN

The original Romantic

Today, people all over the world sing the theme of the final movement of Ludwig van Beethoven's *Symphony No. 9*. You might know it as "Ode to Joy", "Happy Song", "Joyful Joyful", or in the original German, "An die Freude". It's amazing to think that this symphony was composed when Ludwig was almost completely deaf, but he wasn't always unable to hear.

Ludwig started composing at a very young age, pushed by his father who wanted him to be as successful and profitable as the young Wolfgang Amadeus Mozart. In addition to composing, Ludwig was a virtuoso keyboard player, creating new music for the developing piano. He even participated in public piano duels where he faced challengers from near and far—always winning.

Sadly, his performance career ended early when he started to lose his hearing. Though Ludwig stopped performing, he never stopped composing and learned to hear music entirely in his head. As one of Vienna's most famous composers, Ludwig hid his hearing loss from the public for as long as possible, suffering silently and becoming more and more antisocial as his deafness progressed. You can imagine how difficult it is to compose music without being able to hear, but Ludwig channeled his disability to become his strength.

Much of Ludwig's life was turbulent due to the unstable politics of his time. The ideals of the French and American revolutions impacted Ludwig throughout his life, often finding their way into his music. He created music that embodied revolutionary ideals, pushing the limits of what the instruments could play and his audience could understand in his time. When he died, Ludwig was Vienna's most famous composer with over 20,000 people attending his funeral.

FRANZ SCHUBERT

1797 – 1828

VIENNA (AUSTRIA)

FRANZ
SCHUBERT

Vienna's hit-maker

The last meal Franz Schubert ever ate was a fish dinner—a very ironic meal for the composer of "The Trout", a song he first composed for voice and piano and later turned into a quintet for strings and piano.

Though Franz died tragically young, in his short 31 years he composed over 1,000 works including symphonies, operas, chamber music, and hundreds of short songs. His songs were meant to entertain and amuse his friends during a time when if you wanted to hear music, you had to play it yourself. Franz could often be found partying with friends until late in the evening singing songs and sharing music, poetry, and lots of laughs. He was so much fun that the word *Schubertiade* was coined for the gatherings where he would entertain and share music from the piano. These quickly became the parties that everyone wanted to get invited to and where many of his beloved songs premiered.

His songs were sometimes written as stand-alone pieces (one could say these were the first pop song singles) or as cycles (like a modern-day album), such as *Winterreise* and *Die schöne Müllerin*. These songs made Franz the heir apparent to Vienna's musical scene after Ludwig van Beethoven's death in 1827. Unfortunately, it was a role that he would not live long enough to embrace. Franz looked up to Beethoven and was even one of the pallbearers at his funeral, but his health took a turn for the worse only a year after Beethoven's death. The two are buried next to each other and Franz's last request was to hear a performance of Beethoven's 14th string quartet.

THE SCHUMANNS

CLARA SCHUMANN

1819 – 1896

LEIPZIG (GERMANY)

ROBERT SCHUMANN

1810 – 1856

ZWICKAU (GERMANY)

CLARA & ROBERT SCHUMANN

The 19th century's musical power couple

Clara and Robert Schumann were the Beyoncé and Jay-Z of the 19th century. A child prodigy, Clara's skills as a pianist were known far and wide. She was taught by her strict father who was so famous for his piano pedagogy that Robert moved to Leipzig to study with him as a teenager. Several years later, Robert and Clara fell in love, but were forbidden to marry by Clara's father who felt that Robert was not good enough for his superstar daughter. Rebelling, they eloped, becoming one of music's great power couples. As a couple, they built a musical community that outlasted even themselves through their performances, compositions, musical criticism, and support of the next generation of musicians.

Unusual for the time, Clara was the breadwinner of the family, maintaining a busy touring schedule all over Europe and Russia performing works of her own in addition to those of her husband and other composers. Robert's musical career blossomed at a slower pace, and to many in his lifetime, he was known as a music critic and writer rather than a composer. It was Robert's musical newsletter that introduced the world to a young Johannes Brahms who became an extended member of the Schumann family.

Clara, Robert, and their eight children moved several times in support of Robert's career as it grew. Sadly, mental illness cut his life short and he died tragically at the age of 46. In his last days, Robert was visited by Brahms who after Robert's death helped Clara take care of her children while continuing to provide her with musical companionship and support. Clara lived another 40 years after Robert's death, all the while performing and continuing their combined legacy.

GIUSEPPE VERDI

1813 – 1901

LE RONCOLE (ITALY)

GIUSEPPE
VERDI

*Champion of Italian opera whose songs
accompanied a revolution*

At the age of 18, Giuseppe Verdi received a rejection letter from the Music Conservatory of Milan. Devastated at first, he used this rejection as motivation, keeping the letter on his desk for the rest of his life. Giuseppe started from humble beginnings but became one of the richest and most famous Italians in his lifetime, though his path was filled with sorrow. Tragically, Giuseppe's first wife and their two children all died within four years, leaving a sadness in him that found its way into his music.

Giuseppe wrote many famous opera tunes that were hits in his day, including one of his most recognizable songs "La donna è mobile" from the opera *Rigoletto*. Knowing that it would be a hit, Giuseppe didn't let the singer see the music until a few hours before the first performance so that it didn't leak ahead of its premiere. When the public finally heard it, it became incredibly popular and today has found its way into Super Bowl commercials, the video game *Grand Theft Auto*, and even an episode of *The Simpsons*. Giuseppe almost exclusively wrote operas, 28 in his lifetime, that were especially powerful as metaphors for Italian patriotism at a time when Italy was becoming the independent nation we know today. He even got so enthralled in Italian independence and unification that he spent several years serving in Italy's parliament.

Giuseppe died a national hero, receiving an elaborate funeral attended by over 300,000 people. Despite his fame, he preferred to live at his country estate, pouring his wealth into the local community and the estate's buildings, farms, and gardens, even establishing a retirement home for musicians that is still in operation today.

JOHANNES BRAHMS

1833 – 1897

HAMBURG (GERMANY)

JOHANNES BRAHMS

*Vienna's most eligible musical bachelor
with a heart of gold*

Johannes Brahms grew up in a poor musical family, gaining much of his early musical training playing piano in the bars and brothels of Hamburg to help his family make ends meet. Johannes's talents as a composer and performer were recognized early and a series of fortuitous events introduced him to musical power couple Clara and Robert Schumann. This meeting would forever change his life. In Johannes, Robert Schumann saw the future of music and proclaimed this to the world in the music magazine he published, introducing Johannes's music to a wide audience.

Johannes was one of the first composers to seriously study and compile the works of past composers and this work changed his mentality about his own music. While other composers of his time were stretching the boundaries of musical presentation, Johannes focused on stretching the boundaries within traditional forms. He did not focus on volume, but rather quality, completing his first symphony at the age of 43, and destroying many compositions and personal letters before his death.

Johannes never married, living a bachelor's life into old age. Because he could not grow a beard until he was in his 40s, he proudly sported a very large beard for the remainder of his life. Although he was known for dressing poorly, being grumpy, and generally saying what was on his mind without a filter, Johannes also had a heart of gold. When Robert Schumann tragically died, Johannes's friendship with Clara Schumann grew as he stepped in to help raise the Schumann children with Clara, anonymously depositing money in her bank account when she was in need.

Johannes's generosity extended beyond just his friends. While working on his *Symphony No. 4*, a fire broke out in a workshop down the street to which he quickly joined others helping to put out the fire. The fire was contained, and again, Johannes anonymously provided funds for the fire-damaged workshop to be repaired.

LILI'UOKALANI

*Hawai'i's composer Queen who fought for
Hawai'i's culture and independence*

Born in 1838 as part of the extended Hawaiian royal family, Lili'uokalani was not destined to become Queen, but a series of events would lead her to become the first sovereign Queen and last ruler of Hawai'i.

19th century Hawai'i was a rapidly changing place. Colonized by sugar growers and missionaries in the early 1800s, colonists worked to replace native Hawaiian culture with Christianity and the English language. Educated in the royal missionary schools, Lili'uokalani grew up speaking English fluently, but deeply embraced her roots and fought her entire life to preserve and support Hawaiian music, arts, language, and culture. She began composing music that combined Western styles with native Hawaiian musical traditions at a young age and in 1866 composed Hawai'i's national anthem, "He Mele Lāhui Hawai'i", a song in the Hawaiian chant and hymn tradition called Mele. Lili'uokalani wrote more than 150 Mele in her lifetime that encompass the ideals of Aloha: compassion, empathy, and kindness.

During her lifetime, she helped to preserve Hawai'i's most important cultural symbols, built Hawai'i's first hospital, created a savings bank for women and a fund for girls' education, and created a home for Hawaiian orphans that is still in existence today. She remained committed to the ideals of Aloha even after her government was overthrown and she was imprisoned. While imprisoned, Lili'uokalani worked to preserve native Hawaiian legends and history by translating them into English. She also composed music that lamented the treatment of her people and homeland, subversively communicating by publishing the lyrics of her songs embedded with political codes in Hawaiian newspapers. After her release, Lili'uokalani spent the rest of her life advocating for the independence of Hawai'i and for her people, often using her music as a tool for diplomacy.

LILI'UOKALANI

LILI'UOKALANI

1838 – 1917

HONOLULU, HAWAI'I (USA)

CHIQUINHA
GONZAGA

The first pianist of choro

Francisca Edwiges Neves Gonzaga, a.k.a. the famous Chiquinha Gonzaga, was a composer, performer, and activist who took Brazil, and the world, by storm with her music and trailblazing attitudes toward society, equality, and love. However, she suffered great hardships in her fight for happiness and freedom.

Chiquinha was an iconoclast from birth. She was born in 1847 to parents who bucked the taboos of interracial marriage that were prevalent in the 19th century. Her upbringing in a wealthy military family allowed Chiquinha an education worthy of an aristocrat's daughter that included her favorite subject, music. As her musical career blossomed, she experimented with fusing together European musical traditions with popular musical forms of Brazil, becoming an instrumental part of the development of the Brazilian "choro" musical style. This unique blend of music from Europe, Africa, and the Americas is still popular today and considered the heart and soul of Brazilian music. Chiquinha is, in fact, considered the "first pianist of choro"—an extraordinary achievement for a woman of mixed race during a time when women and people of color were not given the respect of their white male peers. Defying societal norms, Chiquinha became the first female conductor in Brazil, founded the Brazilian Society of Theater Authors to protect the intellectual copyright of Brazilian creators, fought for the abolition of slavery, and campaigned for women's right to vote in Brazil. In a radical move for the time, Chiquinha chose to leave several unhappy marriages to men who did not support her music making, eventually meeting the love of her life at age 52, João Batista Fernandes Lage, who worked to preserve and carry on her legacy after her death.

CHIQUINHA GONZAGA

1847 – 1935

RIO DE JANEIRO (BRAZIL)

GUSTAV MAHLER

*Conductor who built his own world
within the symphony*

When Gustav Mahler was four years old, he stumbled upon a piano at his grandparents' house and became instantly infatuated. Gustav didn't have the happiest childhood. He lost eight of his brothers and sisters to illness and had an abusive father. He was also Jewish at a time when Austrian society was very anti-Semitic. Music became the place where Gustav could build his own world and escape his reality, becoming one of the most famous and sought-after composers and conductors of his time.

In his lifetime, Gustav was known as a conductor more than a composer, even spending time in the United States as the conductor of both the Metropolitan Opera and the New York Philharmonic. Immersed in the world of operas and orchestras, Gustav became a master of color and orchestration, writing most of his works for large ensembles of performers. He incorporated unusual instruments and called for experimental staging and techniques. Many of his symphonies have biographical tendencies, incorporating his love for nature, folk songs, marches from his childhood, and memorials to those he lost.

In 1902, Gustav won the hand of Vienna's most eligible bachelorette, Alma Schindler, who was a composer and an intellectual who captured the admiration of many artistic men throughout her life. Although their marriage lasted only nine years until Gustav's death in 1911, Alma outlived him by 51 years, helping to shape his legacy as a composer. As a leading musical figure of his day, Gustav supported and defended innovative younger composers such as Arnold Schoenberg, who several decades later became neighbors with Alma in Los Angeles.

GUSTAV MAHLER

1860 – 1911

KALIŠTĚ (CZECH REPUBLIC)

CLAUDE
DEBUSSY

The musical painter who conjured the clouds and the sea from the tip of his pen

Radical thinking and open-mindedness were encouraged in Claude Debussy's family. Having served time in prison for involvement in the failed Parisian revolution of 1871, Claude's father found his son's first piano teacher through a fellow inmate. It worked out, and Claude entered the Paris Conservatory at the age of ten, excelling as a pianist and composer. From his early days, Claude's creativity led him to create bold ways to move between harmonies, textures, and color, heavily influenced by contemporary poets who sought to focus on art that represented not the physicality of life, but rather the emotions and essence of life.

From his solo piano works like *Clair de lune* to his large orchestral masterpieces like *La mer*, Claude challenged tradition while also building on it. His music captured awe in his audiences for its ability to express so many things that cannot be held: moonlight, clouds, the sea, and dreams. His musical descriptions are so expressive that they leave listeners with the feeling that a cloud just passed through their fingers or they themselves were a boat tossing in the waves of the ocean.

So much of Claude's musical exploration began in 1889 when the world's fair came to Paris, allowing Parisians to hear music they previously never imagined existed. At this fair, a 27-year-old Claude heard gamelan music of Indonesia which he described as being able to express "every shade of meaning, even those one cannot name." We can only imagine how revelatory hearing this music must have been for Claude, inspiring him to search for radical new ways of musical expression that would influence and inspire not only his contemporaries, but generations to come.

CLAUDE DEBUSSY

1862 – 1918

SAINT-GERMAIN-EN-LAYE (FRANCE)

ERIK SATIE

*The late bloomer who marched
to the beat of his own drum*

We often think of great composers as childhood prodigies, but from time to time an example like Erik Satie comes along to remind us that late bloomers can be just as inspirational and effective.

Failing out of school twice by his early 20s, Erik made a living playing the piano in the cafes and nightclubs of Paris. He embraced cultural reform and all things anti-establishment, surrounded by the who's-who of late 19th century Paris. Mingling with so many characters of the Belle Époque, Erik developed a unique personal fashion, sporting a signature velvet suit, top hat, and umbrella. His wildly wonderful style complemented the distinctive music he was writing including his dreamy *Gymnopédies* for piano that floated outside traditional compositional forms.

Without formal training, Erik was free to dream up fantastical music that ventured outside of traditional limits. He incorporated everyday items such as typewriters and sirens in some works and asked a performer to repeat a piece 840 times in another. Regretting not taking his education seriously the first time, Erik eventually returned to school at the age of 38, graduating eight years later with a much more robust toolset to express his unique compositional voice. His theatrical nature led to collaborations with visual artist Pablo Picasso on the ballet *Parade*. He even wrote one of the first film scores. Thanks to the support of friends and fellow composers Maurice Ravel and Claude Debussy, his music was discovered, and he found himself in demand as a composer for the first time at the age of 45.

Despite his flamboyant spirit, music, and dress, Erik was a very private person, never inviting anyone into his apartment. After his death, several friends entered his home and discovered an organized chaos that included two grand pianos stacked on top of each other, the bottom for playing and the top for storage, and over 100 umbrellas. To this day, nobody knows how he stacked the pianos by himself.

ERIK SATIE

1866 – 1925

HONFLEUR (FRANCE)

HARRY T. BURLEIGH

The voice of America who brought Spirituals to the concert stage

It was not long after Antonín Dvořák, the newly appointed director of the National Conservatory of Music, arrived in New York City from Europe that he encountered one of the most beautiful sounds he had ever heard: Harry T. Burleigh singing Spirituals. It was through Harry's mother Elizabeth and his grandfather Hamilton that he learned the rich catalog of African-American Spirituals. Surrounded by music-making at home and at church, Harry became one of Erie, Pennsylvania's most sought-after young performers, which he balanced with various jobs to make ends meet and help support his family.

At 26, Harry entered the most prestigious music school in the country, the National Conservatory of Music in New York City. There he would meet and share the songs he had learned from his family with the famous Czech composer Dvořák who loved hearing Harry sing the Spirituals he had learned from his family. Dvořák felt these Spirituals contained the American musical spirit and so much possibility that he incorporated their influence into his ninth symphony, *From the New World*.

By the end of his time at the National Conservatory, Harry began to create art song arrangements of Spirituals, publishing hundreds throughout his lifetime that became staples of vocal repertoire and brought Spirituals to the concert hall. Harry stayed in New York City for the rest of his career, becoming one of the most famous singers of his time. He wrote his own original music, served as a church music director, and continued to advocate for the inclusion of Spirituals in the classical tradition. He was a beacon in the New York music scene and today, you can witness his legacy at the intersection of East 16th Street and 3rd Avenue, named Harry T. Burleigh Place.

BURLEIGH

HARRY T. BURLEIGH

1866 – 1949

ERIE, PENNSYLVANIA (USA)

JOPLIN

SCOTT JOPLIN

1868 – 1917

MARSHALL, TEXAS (USA)

SCOTT JOPLIN

The King of Ragtime

The "Maple Leaf Rag" was one of the biggest hits of the early 20th century, selling over a half million copies by 1910 and crowning Scott Joplin the "King of Ragtime". Ragtime was the first uniquely American style of music and would go on to influence popular and classical music for decades. Scott's iconic piano pieces like the "Maple Leaf Rag" and "The Entertainer" have become instantly recognizable, but despite these big commercial successes, Scott's life was full of hardship, struggle, and despair.

Scott was born two years after the end of the Civil War and grew up singing and playing the piano. The first pieces he published for the piano employed a new style of syncopated writing that fused African-American folk music elements with Western classical traditions called "Ragtime" in 1895. Scott quickly became the most famous composer of the popular new genre.

There are a lot of composers who achieve widespread success and fame during their lifetimes, but who are forgotten after their passing. Today, Scott is one of the world's most recognizable composers, but like Johann Sebastian Bach, his music was largely forgotten after his death until musicians unearthed and championed his music decades later.

Scott is most well-known for his piano Rags, but also wrote a piano concerto, a symphony, and two operas, all of which have been lost except for the piano-vocal score of his second opera *Treemonisha*. He spent the last decade of his life trying to get *Treemonisha* performed without success. Scott died in New York City at the age of 48, having never heard *Treemonisha* fully performed. Decades later, the opera would be remounted in full productions after Scott's music was rediscovered in the 1970s, earning him a posthumous Pulitzer Prize.

ARNOLD
SCHOENBERG

The master of twelve, who feared thirteen

While many don't believe in superstition, some buildings still refuse to label their 13th floor and there are those whose lives seem ruled by superstition. Born on September 13, 1874, Arnold Schoenberg lived his life afraid of the number 13. He would avoid the 13th floor of buildings, refused to rent a house with the address 13, and even started numbering measures in his music 12a instead of 13. Despite this fear, Arnold became one of the 20th century's most influential composers, changing the shape of what was to come by harnessing the power of the number 12.

Although Arnold showed a love for music at an early age, his family could afford little by way of formal training, leaving him to be largely self-taught. Arnold's early music showed great command of traditional Western harmony and works like *Transfigured Night* were met with acclaim. However, Arnold sought to take music in a new direction, eventually inventing a way to approach harmony that aimed to give equal weight to all 12 notes used in Western music, allowing for new musical possibilities. This 12 tone music was different to anything people had heard before and was shocking to many in his time, while influencing others and changing the future of music. During his lifetime, both World Wars upended how artists thought about the world and for many, Arnold's music embodied the spirit of the times.

Despite fighting for Germany in World War I, the Nazi party identified Arnold as an enemy of the state because of his Jewish heritage. Fortunately, Arnold was able to escape Germany for the United States, settling first in Boston, then in Los Angeles, where he taught at UCLA. Although often thought of as quite a serious character, Arnold enjoyed a good game of tennis and was an avid painter. No matter how hard he tried though, he couldn't escape the number 13 and in an ironic twist of fate, Arnold died on Friday, the 13th of July 1951, just minutes before midnight.

SCHOENBERG

ARNOLD SCHOENBERG

1874 – 1951

VIENNA (AUSTRIA)

RAVEL

MAURICE RAVEL

1875 – 1937

CIBOURE (FRANCE)

MAURICE RAVEL

The enigmatic master of color

Do you know someone who always seems put together, never a button or a hair out of place? Whether a deception or a reality, Maurice Ravel embodied this stereotype, always dressing to perfection and accounting for every detail. There is even a story about Maurice delaying a concert by 30 minutes so he could have just the right shoes for the occasion. His attention to detail was found in everything he did and most certainly in his music. Maurice became known as a master of orchestration; however, that title misses so much more in his music.

Maurice had a deep connection with his mother his whole life, but his father, a pioneering Swiss auto engineer, may have been the source of Maurice's fascination with precision in his work and life. Maurice's compositional process was slow and methodical as he poured over details, ensuring every note was always in the right place. His fascination with details would lead him to write his groundbreaking orchestral piece *Bolero* in which a single theme repeats 80 times, orchestrated in various combinations, and building to a diabolical crescendo over 15 minutes. It was considered radical, but Maurice was no stranger to experimentation and innovation. He was open to new influences, falling in love with jazz after a trip to the United States where he spent nights visiting New York City jazz clubs with George Gershwin. He later incorporated jazz influences into many of his pieces, including his *Piano Concerto in G* and his *Violin Sonata*.

Maurice lived a private life. He never married and spent much of his later life in a home he designed in the country outside of Paris. Because Maurice was private, some accused him of being artificial, to which he famously responded, "Does it not occur to people that I may be artificial by nature?"

SAMUEL COLERIDGE-TAYLOR

English champion of the African diaspora

Like Wolfgang Amadeus Mozart and Franz Schubert, Samuel Coleridge-Taylor wrote a remarkable amount of music and had an outsized impact on the musical world despite dying at the young age of 37.

It was only after Samuel's father had left England to return to his home in Sierra Leone that his mother found out she was pregnant with Samuel. Sadly, he would never meet his father, but his profound pride in his African descent would greatly influence his music. Samuel's grandfather taught him how to play the violin and ensured he had access to England's best musical schools as both a violinist and a composer. Samuel's talents were obvious to all who knew him, and he became an international celebrity upon the publication of his musical trilogy based on the poem of Henry Wadsworth Longfellow, *The Song of Hiawatha*. Published before the first performance, the first part of the piece was a hit and Samuel was commissioned to write a sequel even before anyone had heard a single note! After finally being performed, it was considered one of the most remarkable musical successes of a generation. It became a national and international sensation that rivaled George Frideric Handel's *Messiah* in popularity and even led to three tours of the United States where a whole new nation of people fell in love with his music.

Samuel developed a profound respect and love for African-American music that he incorporated into his work. Fellow iconic composer Harry T. Burleigh sang in the Washington, D.C., performance of *The Song of Hiawatha* with Samuel himself conducting, leading to a friendship and mutual admiration between the two composers. Though he would forever be immortalized as the composer of *The Song of Hiawatha*, Samuel wrote for orchestra, chamber music, operas, and ballets in addition to teaching, conducting, and researching and promoting the music and works of the African diaspora.

COLERIDGE-TAYLOR

SAMUEL COLERIDGE-TAYLOR

1875 – 1912

LONDON, ENGLAND (UK)

IGOR STRAVINSKY

The musical chameleon who started a riot and created an iconic hip-hop sample

Sometimes compositions premiere before audiences are quite ready for them. After composing two successful ballets, Igor Stravinsky premiered his third, *The Rite of Spring*, in 1913, to what was described as a riot. At the premiere, the audience shouted and hurled items. Fights broke out and many attendees were arrested for their reactions to the music and dance. Some instantly understood the brilliance of the work, while others clearly needed time to adapt. This same piece that caused such a fuss in 1913 was presented in Disney's animated film *Fantasia* in 1940 as the only work by a living composer, showing just how quickly tastes can change.

Igor experienced tremendous change in his lifetime. He lived through two World Wars, and moved from his native Russia to Switzerland, then France, eventually settling in the United States, fleeing war and seeking opportunity. He spent the last 32 years of his life in the United States, becoming a U.S. citizen in 1945. Called "the chameleon" by some for his ability to adapt musically, Igor's compositional style would evolve throughout his life, developing into three distinct periods. His early period balanced Romantic and Russian folk influences mixed with his own unique sense of rhythm, form, and juxtaposition. Igor's second phase, often labeled neoclassical, looked back to earlier influences and culminated in his opera *The Rake's Progress*. After years of antagonizing each other publicly, Igor entered his third period, embracing the 12-tone system created by Arnold Schoenberg.

Igor's fame grew throughout his lifetime. He was honored on his 80th birthday by President John F. Kennedy, was called the "greatest composer of our time" by Leonard Bernstein, and received a posthumous Grammy for lifetime achievement. He even has a star on the Hollywood Walk of Fame. In an unexpected turn, a one-second clip from his *Firebird Suite* dubbed the "Orchestra Hit" became an iconic sample used in countless pop and hip-hop songs from the 1980s to today by artists including Bruno Mars, Prince, Madonna, Janet Jackson, N.W.A. and many more.

IGOR STRAVINSKY

1882 – 1971

LOMONOSOV (RUSSIA)

FLORENCE PRICE

1887 – 1953

LITTLE ROCK, ARKANSAS (USA)

FLORENCE PRICE

The first Black woman to be recognized as a symphonic composer

In 2009, a couple bought an abandoned home in St. Anne, Illinois, that had been left unoccupied since 1953. In the only room where the roof had not collapsed, they discovered boxes of handwritten manuscripts. The music belonged to Florence Price, who had left it there expecting to return.

Having graduated as the valedictorian of her high school class by the age of 14, Florence enrolled as a pianist and composer far from her hometown of Little Rock, Arkansas, at Boston's New England Conservatory of Music. Graduating with degrees in organ performance and music education, Florence returned to Little Rock where she taught music, met her husband, and had two children, but it was not to last. Racial violence had erupted in her hometown and the Price family were forced to move north to escape the impact of Jim Crow laws, settling in Chicago. It was in Chicago that Florence found a community of like-minded artists that supported her musical growth in the face of adverse personal struggles.

After a bitter divorce, Florence supported herself and her children, making ends meet by teaching over 100 piano students while also finding time to build her career as a composer. After years of fighting for recognition, Florence's *Symphony No. 1* was premiered by the Chicago Symphony Orchestra, becoming the first composition by a Black female composer to be performed by a major orchestra in the United States. Her music incorporated many influences, including elements of church music and Spirituals interwoven with traditional classical forms and counterpoint.

In 1953, Florence was scheduled to tour her music throughout Europe, but tragically suffered a stroke, dying suddenly before she was able to see her music played around the world. She would never return to her summer home where her pieces of unpublished music, including a symphony and several concertos, lay abandoned until their discovery in 2009. Since then, these rediscovered works have been performed to much fanfare and acclaim.

THE BOULANGERS

LILI BOULANGER
1893 – 1918
PARIS (FRANCE)

NADIA BOULANGER
1887 – 1979
PARIS (FRANCE)

LILI & NADIA
BOULANGER

Sisters that encouraged future generations
of composers to find their unique voices

In 1913, Lili Boulanger became the first woman to win the Rome Prize, the highest honor a student composer could earn at the Paris Conservatory. Lili and her older sister, Nadia, were both talented pianists and composers who had big hopes for their futures, but misfortune would change everything. Lili suffered from poor respiratory health her whole life and tragically died at the age of 24. She did so much with little time, composing over 50 pieces while also spending much of her final years helping wounded soldiers during the first World War.

The loss of Lili affected Nadia dramatically. After Lili's death, Nadia stopped composing to focus on teaching, conducting, and promoting her sister's works. Nadia's ability as a conductor and a teacher was quickly recognized. As her reputation grew, composers and performers from all over the world came to Nadia's studio to learn her techniques of hearing, looking, listening, and seeing. Nadia shaped the music and lives of an unbelievable list of composers including Aaron Copland, Philip Glass, Quincy Jones, and Astor Piazzolla, encouraging each one to pursue his or her individual voice. She humbly credited her success as a teacher to the quality of her students. Her lineage can be tied directly and indirectly to thousands of musicians all over the world.

In addition to her rigorous method of teaching, Nadia befriended the who's who of the composers of her day and conducted the premieres of major works by Igor Stravinsky, Francis Poulenc, and many others. As a conductor, Nadia changed the minds of many who believed women could not lead orchestras, becoming the first woman to lead the New York Philharmonic, Boston Symphony Orchestra, and Royal Philharmonic Orchestra. Living to the age of 92, Nadia saw two World Wars and women gain suffrage throughout the world. For many, she proved women can command equal respect as men and has been called the "most influential teacher since Socrates."

WILLIAM GRANT STILL

*Member of the Harlem Renaissance
who left an indelible mark on American music*

Every day, William Grant Still put on a three-piece suit and wingtip shoes to go and work in his composition studio, creating richly colorful works on his special typewriter that had music notes instead of letters. William had a great sense of humor, and always kept a puzzle book by his bed, fitting for a composer who excelled at the musical puzzle of orchestration—choosing which instrument would perfectly fit each line of music. William's knowledge of so many different instruments made him really good at orchestration. So good, in fact, that George Gershwin sought him out for orchestration lessons.

William graduated high school as valedictorian at just 16 years old. While he initially chose to study pre-med, he eventually transferred to Oberlin Conservatory of Music where he deepened his musical studies. Upon graduation, he got a job in Memphis working for W.C. Handy, known as the "father of the blues," before joining the Navy to serve in World War I. He would return to work for W.C. Handy after the war, but this time in New York City, where William became a part of the flowering Harlem Renaissance.

William was an entrepreneur, working for W.C. Handy, playing in Broadway musicals, and serving as the musical director of the first Black-owned record company, Black Swan. He continued studying classical music composition with such luminaries as avant-garde composer Edgard Varèse, who championed William's music and secured William's first big commission. William would go on to write and arrange music for numerous television shows and movies in addition to writing concert works which he conducted all over the world. His music touched almost every style, from popular to symphonic, and when the 1939 World's Fair held a competition to write its theme music William sent in three submissions, all anonymously. The judges could not decide between the top two submissions, and when they unveiled the two finalists, they turned out to both be by William.

WILLIAM GRANT STILL

1895 – 1978

WOODVILLE, MISSISSIPPI (USA)

GRAHAM DU BOIS

SHIRLEY GRAHAM DU BOIS

1896 – 1977

INDIANAPOLIS, INDIANA (USA)

SHIRLEY GRAHAM DU BOIS

*Activist-composer whose opera
sold out a baseball stadium*

Shirley Graham Du Bois had one big performance, and it was about as big as you could get. It was 1932 and over two nights, 25,000 people packed into a baseball stadium in Cleveland, Ohio, to hear Shirley's new opera, *Tom-Tom*, and then it was never heard again. Preserved in the Harvard University archives, scholars and opera companies have been working to reintroduce the piece to audiences but experiencing the full opera as it was premiered in 1932 is a serious undertaking. The original production was magnificent, involving an all-Black cast, 200-person chorus, full orchestra, live elephant, and even a waterfall on stage.

Moving from town to town due to her father's job as a preacher, Shirley was comfortable engaging with the communities around her. At 13 years old, Shirley witnessed racial inequity firsthand after being denied entry to a neighborhood pool, starting her storied career in activism with a letter to the local newspaper protesting the discrimination. Though she married and had two children in her 20s, Shirley never stopped furthering her education, attending the Sorbonne, Columbia University, Howard University, and Oberlin Conservatory, where she premiered *Tom-Tom* as a student. The opera incorporated a wide array of musical influences, bringing to life a three-act story subtitled *The Epic of Music and the Negro* that chronicled the African diaspora from pre-colonial West Africa to 1920s Harlem. Shirley combined elements of West African drumming, Spirituals, early jazz, sounds of New York City, and more into her production.

Though Shirley would continue to compose after *Tom-Tom*, her career in writing and political activism took center stage, eventually bringing her together with her second husband and fellow activist, W.E.B. Du Bois, with whom she worked tirelessly to combat oppression, fight for Black liberation, and improve human and civil rights for people around the world.

GEORGE GERSHWIN

1898 – 1937

NEW YORK, NEW YORK (USA)

GEORGE
GERSHWIN

*The American who brought jazz from
New York to Paris and back*

When George Gershwin's parents bought a piano for their home, they imagined it was going to be for their son Ira, but on the day of its arrival they were shocked when their younger son George became instantly infatuated. Ira and George would become lifelong collaborators and were eventually recruited to Hollywood, but as a child, George was a poor student in Brooklyn who showed little interest in anything but music. To his parents' disappointment, George dropped out of school at the age of 15 to start working in the music business, selling other people's sheet music on New York City's Tin Pan Alley. George wanted to do more than just sell music and decided to try his hand at songwriting and composing in addition to dabbling in new technologies like creating piano rolls that allowed people to have automated performances outside the concert hall.

Absorbing much of the popular influences of the day, specifically jazz, George wrote his first hit, *Swanee*, at the age of 21. This was followed by *Rhapsody in Blue*, which became an instant hit and planted George in both the popular and art music worlds. As his fame grew and he traveled the world, he would meet with Maurice Ravel, Nadia Boulanger, and many other influential composers of his day to seek advice. However, they refused to take him on as a student as they didn't want to change his already unique and successful compositional voice, with Ravel famously saying, "Why become a second-rate Ravel when you're already a first-rate Gershwin?" He would forever immortalize his time in Paris in his jazzy orchestral piece, *An American in Paris*.

George moved to Los Angeles as a musical star, writing music for Hollywood films and playing tennis with Arnold Schoenberg weekly, but the games weren't to last. In February 1937, George lost consciousness at the piano in the middle of a concert. His health deteriorated in the ensuing months, dying at the age of 38 as one of America's most famous composers.

JOHN
CAGE

*The 20th century's musical philosopher
who took a chance on silence*

In 1952, there was a world premiere of a new piece in three movements called
4'33" that began with a pianist walking on stage, closing the piano lid…and just
sitting there. Between movements, the pianist opened the lid and closed it again
to signal the start of the next movement. The entire piece had not a single written
note, but simply four minutes and 33 seconds of silence accompanied by the rustle
of confused audience members and other ambient noise. This piece was one of
many works by John Cage that challenged traditional conceptions of what music,
and a composer, was.

John was surrounded by people who thought about things differently, from
his first teacher, Arnold Schoenberg, to his friend, Dada artist Marcel Duchamp,
and his teachers of Eastern philosophy. The convergence of these influences gave
John the freedom to redefine what it meant to be a composer and what music
itself was. Controversial in his time, John's music remains a topic of debate and
inspiration for composers, performers, and philosophers today.

John was fascinated with new sounds and unusual approaches to creating
music. He had a love for percussion, and his open-minded attitude led him to
find music in formerly untapped sources, such as cacti quills, conch shells, and
the sound of fire. He even placed objects inside the piano itself, transforming
the instrument into something resembling a percussion ensemble rather than
a piano. At the heart of his work was spontaneity and collaboration, whether
with performers or with other creators, like dancer and choreographer Merce
Cunningham, who became John's lifelong partner. The pair inspired each other
to allow the randomness of chance to drive their creative output and inspired
others to search for innovative ways to engage with music and life.

JOHN CAGE

1912 – 1992

LOS ANGELES, CALIFORNIA (USA)

LEONARD
BERNSTEIN

New York's musical ambassador

The U.S. born son of Ukrainian Jewish immigrants, Leonard Bernstein was driven, charming, gifted, and lucky. Everyone called him Lenny. He received his big break at the age of 25, stepping in at the last minute to replace a sick conductor in a live national broadcast with his future orchestra, the New York Philharmonic. Lenny became famous overnight. Like Gustav Mahler, whose music he revived and championed, Lenny pursued the tricky balance of being both a conductor and a composer. Fortunately, Lenny didn't sleep much, so he found time amidst his busy conducting schedule to churn out masterpieces for the concert hall, dance stage, opera house, Broadway, and more.

Lenny was informal and fun, and he loved to share all kinds of music with all kinds of audiences—including on television: his Young People's Concerts with the New York Philharmonic delighted and inspired millions of viewers worldwide. A passionate educator, Lenny found exciting ways to captivate audiences young and old about music from centuries past all the way to brand-new works.

One of Lenny's most iconic pieces is his musical, *West Side Story*. Less than two years after the premiere of *West Side Story*, the New York City neighborhood where the action takes place began to be transformed into Lincoln Center for the Performing Arts. Lincoln Center became the new home for Lenny's orchestra, the New York Philharmonic.

Whenever he could, Lenny used his music-making to reach across social and political barriers. After the fall of the Berlin Wall in 1989, he was moved to celebrate the city's newfound freedom with a globally broadcast performance of Ludwig van Beethoven's immortal *Ninth Symphony*. In a touch typical of Lenny's charm, he modified the famous "Ode to Joy" chorus to become an "Ode to Freedom."

BERNSTEIN

LEONARD BERNSTEIN

1918 – 1990

LAWRENCE, MASSACHUSETTS (USA)

USTVOLSKAYA

GALINA USTVOLSKAYA

1919 – 2006

ST. PETERSBURG (RUSSIA)

GALINA USTVOLSKAYA

Elusive composer who would not be defined

When asked what she wanted to be when she grew up, Galina Ustvolskaya replied, "an orchestra." Throughout her life, she poured every ounce of her energy, heart, mind, and being into her music, expecting the same dedication from her listeners. Galina felt the ideal place for performances of her music was not in a concert hall, but in a church or a temple. She did not consider her work religious, but felt she was devoted to spiritual, non-religious creativity, sometimes taking seven or eight years to complete a piece.

Galina was constantly composing *something*, though she was very particular about what would end up included in her catalog, cautiously guarding which works made it into the public arena. At the time of her death, she had destroyed all but 21 works, wanting only the music that met her high standards to survive in the world outside her own head. A well-known recluse, Galina rarely spoke about her music, building her own musical world and compositional voice that bears no resemblance to anyone but Galina herself.

Galina used instrumental combinations that might seem unusual for other composers but that perfectly fit the demands of each of her pieces. A trio for piccolo, tuba, and piano; an octet of two oboes, four violins, timpani, and piano; a group of eight double basses, a piano, and her signature "cube", a 43cm x 43cm percussion instrument made of 2cm thick chipboard she designed for its specific sound.

Galina's music, especially her piano works, are extremely demanding of the performer, taking a huge amount of physical strength and endurance with stories of bleeding fingers and knuckles during and after performances of her music. Despite this, Galina also had a soft side. She was particularly fond of chocolate-covered prunes, loved the color red, and felt that nature, silence, and rest were the most important things in life.

ASTOR
PIAZZOLLA

The tango evolutionist

When you meddle with a symbol of national pride, things can get hairy. Astor Piazzolla found out the hard way when a taxi driver refused him service because he "killed the tango."

Born in Argentina, Astor's family moved to New York City when he was only four years old. His father would share Argentine tango to teach Astor about his homeland. Astor loved it. One day, Astor's father spotted a bandoneón, an accordion-like tango instrument popular in Argentina, in the window of a New York City pawn shop and Astor's fate was sealed. He fell in love with the instrument and practiced so hard that by the time the family moved back to Argentina in 1936, Astor was playing with some of the country's best tango musicians even though he was only 15 years old, catapulting him to musical fame in his home country.

Balancing his career as a tango musician, Astor built a foundation in traditional composition with Alberto Ginastera, who encouraged him to go to Paris to study with Nadia Boulanger in order to move beyond his tango roots, expanding his musical palette and assimilating current musical trends. Boulanger was not one to beat around the bush and did not favor the music he showed her until she saw his tangos, which she encouraged wholeheartedly. This affirmation pushed him to focus on nothing but tango, believing it was the foundation of his true compositional voice. Astor would return to Argentina with a renewed passion, infusing the tango with classical and jazz influences, taking the tango out of the dance hall and bringing it to the concert stage.

Astor spent the remainder of his life writing what he called "new tangos," slowly building admiration for his work as he performed all over the world. Even the most traditional tango lover in Argentina would eventually grow to love Astor's music, transforming him from a villain trying to destroy the tango to a national hero.

PIAZZOLLA

ASTOR PIAZZOLLA

1921 – 1992

MAR DEL PLATA (ARGENTINA)

CRUMB

GEORGE CRUMB

1929 – 2022

CHARLESTON, WEST VIRGINIA (USA)

GEORGE
CRUMB

The Appalachian composer who
wrote music from his heart

Unlike Arnold Schoenberg, George Crumb grabbed the number 13 by the horns and harnessed its power in his electric string quartet *Black Angels, Thirteen Images from the Dark Land*, finished on Friday, March 13, 1970. The wildly stirring work reflects the terrors of the Vietnam War, illustrating the fight between good and evil with riveting sonic effects created through unconventional uses of the string quartet. Always one to go beyond the traditional expectations of the concert hall, George took his influences from nature, history, and politics, asking performers to do more than just play their instruments: moving about the stage, donning theatrical costumes, amplifying, speaking, whistling, and employing a variety of unusual objects to create his other-worldly, timeless sounds.

Though George's style was fiercely independent, he was not one to eschew history, often incorporating short snippets of pieces by earlier composers into his works in haunting ways. Artistically, he was the continuation of an elaborate notational school of composers with origins in 14th century France who strove to take their music to a new level by presenting their manuscripts in beautiful shapes from hearts to harps. Six centuries later, George felt his music "should look the way it sounds" and continued this tradition, creating handwritten manuscripts whose designs inspired the imaginations of performers by taking the form of a spiral, an eye, a peace sign, and more.

While looking at and listening to his music might give the impression that George had a serious character, he was famously down to earth, often telling jokes in his unmistakably warm and approachable West Virginia accent. George composed until his death at 92 years old, constantly looking for new sounds and striving to write the type of music that he wanted to write in his "heart of hearts."

TŌRU TAKEMITSU

1930 – 1996

TOKYO (JAPAN)

TŌRU
TAKEMITSU

The composer who was one with the stream of sound

Just a few days before his death, Tōru Takemitsu sent a postcard to pianist Peter Serkin wishing for the strong body of a whale to swim in an ocean "that has no west and no east." Tōru had spent much of his life as a cultural bridge between Eastern and Western music and philosophy, wanting not only to blend Western and Japanese music, but to "confront those contradictions, even intensify them."

Coming of age in Japan in the aftermath of World War II, Tōru had his childhood stripped away from him. He was conscripted to work on a military base where any Western media, language, and especially music was forbidden. One day, an older soldier shared with him a French song that transformed his life. Consumed with becoming a musician, Tōru desperately wanted a piano, but buying one was out of the question, so he fashioned a replica keyboard out of paper that he could fold up and carry around with him. As thrilled as he was when he finally got his hands on a real piano, for Tōru, the paper piano was capable of far greater sounds and possibility than the real thing.

Over the course of his career, Tōru wrote hundreds of musical works, scored more than 90 films, and wrote 20 books. Nature was hugely important to Tōru who derived much of his compositional outlook from Zen philosophy where one's self is inextricable from the surrounding world and nature itself. Tōru was a composer who didn't use sounds, he collaborated with them, viewing music as a form of prayer and composition as a stream with which he was one. He dedicated his entire career to collaborating with the many sounds of nature, life, and dreams, always striving to be able to speak the language of sound in the way that sound itself spoke.

LEE

YOUNG-JA LEE

Born 1931

WONJU (KOREA)

YOUNG-JA LEE

The godmother of Korean modern music

Young-ja Lee was in the middle of a master's degree when the Korean War broke out. She walked for three days to her hometown but her family was nowhere to be found. Sheltering in an abandoned house for months, malnourished and in fear, she wondered what life would be like after the war. She prayed to the sky asking for guidance. What should she do with her life if she survived? She decided to become a composer to put into music all of her life experiences, the challenges, and the joys, bringing peace and love to those who are heartbroken.

After the war, Young-ja returned to school. She had fallen in love with music at ten years old and now her path after the war was not only as a pianist, but also as a composer. Eager to learn more, Young-ja traveled to Europe and the United States, furthering her education at the Royal Conservatory in Brussels, the Manhattan School of Music in New York, and in France at the Sorbonne and the Paris Conservatory, where she studied with composer Olivier Messiaen. She would bring all these experiences back with her to Korea, returning to her alma mater, Ewha Women's University, to teach generations of female composers, leaving an indelible mark on new music in Korea.

Young-ja's music fuses elements of music from around the world, writing for both Western and Korean instruments. Young-ja was greatly influenced by the music that she heard during her travels abroad as a student and later in life with her husband who worked as a diplomat. Their family spent time in Belgium, the Ivory Coast, Indonesia, and France, Young-ja absorbing the musical sounds in each place, feeling that music was more than just notes. Her music encompasses everything from the crash of breaking windows to the sounds of horse hooves, fights, and more. Her passion for composing has never waned, writing hundreds of works and still spending 10-12 hours a day, and sometimes all night, composing.

LOUIS W. BALLARD

The composer who stood with eagles

In the late 19th century, the U.S. government created a network of boarding schools whose mission was to eradicate American Indian culture and language by taking children away from their tribes, families, and traditions. It was at one of these boarding schools that a six-year-old Louis W. Ballard was punished for speaking his tribal languages and performing the tribal dances he had grown up with as a member of the Quapaw and Cherokee nations. Louis didn't stay at the school long but would continue to move between worlds for the rest of his life, working tirelessly to preserve, share, and expand upon American Indian music while also unifying it with Western musical traditions in his own music.

Away from the boarding school, Louis excelled in high school, where he learned to play the piano, sing, dance, was captain of the football and baseball teams, and graduated as valedictorian of his class. Louis was the first American Indian recipient of a master's degree in composition from his university, and saw cultural differences as an opportunity for cultural enrichment. He worked to preserve and promote the Quapaw traditions as a member of the War Dance Society of the Quapaw tribe, and later as the music director for the Institute of American Indian Arts. At the Institute, he formed the American Indian Creative Percussion Ensemble and the E-Yah-Pah-Hah Indian Chanters who performed American Indian songs that Louis arranged.

Louis created a classroom curriculum for teachers and students looking to incorporate American Indian music and, in addition to cataloging and recording music from tribes throughout the United States, Louis published original ballets, cantatas, an opera, and works for piano, orchestra, and chamber ensembles. He spent many summers as a faculty member of the Aspen Music Festival where he met his second wife, Ruth Doré. Together, Ruth and Louis strove to make sure that American Indian musical traditions were celebrated and passed on for generations to come.

BALLARD

LOUIS W. BALLARD

1931 – 2007

MIAMI, OKLAHOMA (USA)

WILLIAMS

JOHN WILLIAMS

Born 1932

NEW YORK, NEW YORK (USA)

JOHN WILLIAMS

*The Hollywood icon who has written
the soundtrack for generations*

In 1975, John Williams terrified the world with only two notes. They begin slowly at first, oscillating back and forth in the lowest register. Gradually, they speed up and set the listener's anxiety racing as the threat of the killer shark, *Jaws*, draws nearer and nearer. This simple theme is just one of many instantly recognizable motives John composed for movies, bringing to life our hopes and fears in as little as two notes.

Though John made his career in Hollywood, he was born in New York City, cutting his teeth in the Air Force where he performed, conducted, arranged music, and wrote his first film score. He would later hone his piano skills as a student at The Juilliard School, but it was not long before John made his way to the West Coast, starting his career as a studio musician in Los Angeles recording other people's film scores. Soon, John would start scoring various films and television shows himself, gaining widespread recognition after winning his first Oscar in 1971. Just one year later, he would begin his decades-long collaboration with filmmaker Steven Spielberg, creating the iconic sounds of such films as *Indiana Jones*, *E.T.*, *Jurassic Park*, *Schindler's List*, *Jaws*, and more. His scores are lush, imaginative, and romantic, bringing a symphonic renaissance to the film score world, drawing inspiration from music of the past, present, and from places and peoples around the world. John's music instantly transports listeners from the far corners of the universe in *Star Wars* to the magical castle of Hogwarts in *Harry Potter*.

In addition to the 25 Grammys, five Oscars, and many other awards John has won for his music, he also conducted the Boston Pops for over a decade. Away from the scoring studio, he can be found conducting concert arrangements of his film scores in addition to his concert works with orchestras, his love for creating distinctive characters ever-present in his favorite medium, the concerto.

PAULINE OLIVEROS

*The composer who transformed
hearing into listening*

In 1988, Pauline Oliveros descended underground into a large human-made chamber once used as a water reservoir. This cistern had something very special: 45 seconds of reverb. Deep underground, Pauline improvised music and the cistern responded back, transforming every sound in new and fascinating ways. Pauline had to listen deeply to figure out how to interact with the environment. She coined the term "deep listening" that day, first as a pun, but then as a guiding force to all her artistic endeavors.

Deep listening implores performers and audience members alike to explore the difference between hearing and listening as a way to tune the mind and body, expanding consciousness and promoting healing. Pauline felt this was as much a humanitarian endeavor as a musical one.

Pauline encouraged people to listen all the time, and to remind oneself when one is not listening. Her musical scores are often written in the form of text, instructing participants in ways to listen and engage with sound, their bodies, and their surroundings:

"Take a walk at night. Walk so silently that the bottoms of your feet become ears."

For one year, she played only one note, an A, delving deep into the possibility of what that single note could express. Though many of her scores require only the human body, her primary instrument was the accordion. She was equally pioneering in the field of electronic music, finding ways to further enhance the voice, instruments, and music making experience with technology, even collaborating on a digital version of the deep listening cistern that allows people to access the breathtaking resonance anywhere in the world.

OLIVEROS

PAULINE OLIVEROS

1932 – 2016

HOUSTON, TEXAS (USA)

ARVO PÄRT

Mystic minimalist of peace and love

After suffering from writer's block for years, a frustrated Arvo Pärt decided to take a walk on a snowy morning. Seeing a street cleaner, a desperate Arvo asked him, "What should a composer do?" The cleaner's response shocked Arvo. "A composer should love every note." This stranger summarized what Arvo had spent eight years building towards.

During this evolutionary time in his life, Arvo converted to Orthodox Christianity, immersed himself in the study of Medieval and Renaissance church music, and even lived at a monastery. He would reemerge with tremendous faith, creating a new minimalist compositional style that blended old and new influences with religious mysticism. Arvo called his new style *Tintinnabuli*, taking inspiration from the bells that would break the silence he experienced at the monastery. This new style focused on two voices—one that he believed represented his sins and the other one forgiveness—in a style that greatly contrasted his previous works which had been heavily influenced by the limited types of music he had had access to in Soviet-controlled Estonia.

As a child, the piano in Arvo's house had a broken middle register, leaving him the upper and lower registers with which to experiment, cementing a lifelong fascination with contrast that he incorporates into his music. Though he received acclaim for his early stage and film works, he only started to gain global recognition after he wiped his musical slate clean, going on to create his most loved pieces of music including *Fratres*, *Tabula Rasa*, and *Cantus in Memory of Benjamin Britten*. Today, Arvo's music is played all over the world and the depth of his music has found a home in many hearts.

ARVO PÄRT

Born 1935

PAIDE (ESTONIA)

PHILIP GLASS

Born 1937

BALTIMORE, MARYLAND (USA)

PHILIP GLASS

The minimalist with the maximum impact

In his mid-30s, Philip Glass was struggling to make ends meet in New York City. He worked as a mover, plumber, and taxi driver, hoping that after the premiere of his opera *Einstein at the Beach* at New York's Metropolitan Opera House, things would be different. One day, as a passenger left his taxi, she exclaimed to him that he shared a name with a famous composer who had just had his opera premiered at the Metropolitan Opera. Philip smiled and thanked her, continuing his day, knowing he would be able to focus on composing full-time sooner rather than later.

Philip grew up playing the flute and piano and at the age of 15 enrolled at the University of Chicago, studying mathematics and philosophy. Deciding music was his calling, he moved to New York to study piano and composition at The Juilliard School, later traveling to Paris to study with esteemed teacher Nadia Boulanger. Within two years, his compositional path would be changed forever as Nadia gave Philip confidence in his fundamental skills. It was in Paris that he met Indian classical music star Ravi Shankar, who Philip collaborated with on a film score, opening Philip's eyes to other types of and perspectives on music that would greatly influence his compositional voice.

Taking this all in, Philip synthesized many types of music. He developed his own minimalist style with an eye for drama that shone particularly bright in his works for the stage and film, in addition to his intimately powerful concert music. Although his music was not accepted by the public at first, it has now become mainstream, copied by many and influencing others. Today Philip continues to be very prolific and sought after as one of the most performed living composers, his productions still selling out the house at the Metropolitan Opera in New York for a new generation of opera lovers.

ROSCOE MITCHELL

*Maestro of sound who creates art
with splashes of color*

Roscoe Mitchell has undeniable style with his signature sunglasses and one-of-a-kind hand-painted suits that are the perfect representation of his music. He is a musician who has changed the course of classical, jazz, and so many more styles of music with his groundbreakingly creative approaches to sound.

Painting outside of the lines has always been a part of Roscoe's character. Growing up in Chicago, he became a pioneering force in the music scene by his early 20s as one of the founding members of the Association for the Advancement of Creative Musicians, a group known as the AACM. The AACM was the creative outlet for young musicians in Chicago looking to nurture, perform, and record serious, original music. It was from within the AACM that Roscoe built his world-famous group, the Art Ensemble of Chicago, or AEC.

Originally, the AEC didn't have a drummer, so instead, members would take turns playing a variety of percussion instruments. Even after they found the perfect percussionist to join them, Roscoe's love for percussion stayed with him. He continued to play percussion with both the AACM and AEC, building highly specialized setups, in addition to his main instrument, the saxophone. His music plays with time, silence, range, and timbre, frequently distorting the sounds of the instruments he is playing to create brand new colors.

He has collaborated with a remarkable number of musicians, and is featured on over 90 albums, often using improvisations from live performances as source material for his written compositions. Also a visual artist, original paintings adorn his studio where he and his wife Wendy collaborate to produce films of his music, showcasing at once just how serious and how playful he is.

ROSCOE MITCHELL
Born 1940
CHICAGO, ILLINOIS (USA)

JULIUS EASTMAN

1940-1990

NEW YORK, NEW YORK (USA)

JULIUS EASTMAN

Minimalist who lived his life to the fullest

You could recognize Julius Eastman's laugh anywhere. Intensely musical, it started as a low bubbling as if from a deep underground spring, bursting forth into the world with rippling waves that extended far and wide. From Julius sprung so much more—works of kaleidoscopic color and feeling that never fail to leave both audience and performer transformed.

After studying at Philadelphia's Curtis Institute of Music, Julius bounced between New York City and Buffalo where he joined the prestigious Creative Associates at the University at Buffalo. The Creative Associates were a group of experimental composer-performers including George Crumb and Pauline Oliveros. As a Creative Associate, Julius created works and performed his and others' music either on the piano, or with his remarkable deep and beautiful voice that was capable of great range and expression. Julius's voice had made an indelible mark on the music community and other composers, but it was Julius's own music where his voice had the freedom to express ebullient joy and defiant rage.

Julius's mission was to be Black, gay, and a musician to the fullest. He was bursting at the seams with music, so much so that sometimes the only place he had to write his musical ideas down was on a cocktail napkin at a bar. Julius's compositions made sure that every performer involved was contributing their full selves to the performance through the way he structured his works with open-ended guidance that allows for individual interpretation, contribution, and structured improvisation. His compositions use stopwatches to deftly coordinate a group of musicians who don't stop pounding eighth notes for over 30 minutes, use text to bring to life a call to action to speak boldly, and one piece is even composed in the shape of an egg. Sadly, much of Julius's work was lost during his life, and more after his death. Today, however, musicians are rediscovering his fantastically bold and impactful voice.

MONK

MEREDITH MONK

Born 1942

NEW YORK, NEW YORK (USA)

MEREDITH MONK

The artist who mined the depths
of the human voice

Meredith Monk's music explores the depths of the human voice, inquiring how it might jump, spin, spiral, and fall, how language forms, and how we communicate with and without recognizable words. Coming from a family of four generations of professional singers, singing was always a part of Meredith's DNA. At a young age, Meredith's mother enrolled her in a special kind of music class, Dalcroze technique, a way to learn and experience music through movement, not knowing the impact this would have on both her daughter and on the performing arts world. The body is the foundation of all Meredith's work, with the voice as the cornerstone.

Meredith creates works that are spiritual at their core. The backbone of her productions is her unique musical and vocal language that speaks to various aspects of society and the world.

Her music has a certain organic nature to it with many pieces written for specific people's voices and bodies. You can frequently find Meredith as part of the ensemble of performers in productions of her work, bringing together a community of generous and kind collaborators she developed to share in, contribute to, and carry on her craft.

Her work often defies traditional categorization, but Meredith has always considered her work of all sizes to be opera, for her, the combination of movement, music, and theater. She has built a momentous body of work throughout her career, from films, to visual artwork, to songs, to fully produced operas.

Music is the river of her life, ever flowing, garnering accolades including a 2015 National Medal of Arts, amongst many others. She is a New York City institution, for many years cheered on by her pet turtle, Neutron, and instantly recognizable with her signature pigtails.

LEÓN

TANIA LEÓN

Born 1943

HAVANA (CUBA)

TANIA LEÓN

The composers' advocate

Tania León was 24 when she left Cuba, stepping onto a plane bound for the United States all alone and speaking not a word of English. It didn't take her long to make waves. Tania loved music, but never imagined that one day she would become a composer, conductor, and ambassador for classical music all over the world. Shortly after arriving in New York City, Tania met legendary dancer Arthur Mitchell who immediately recognized that she had a special musical voice. Together, they founded the Dance Theater of Harlem, and Tania realized that it was composing, not just playing the piano, that was her calling after writing her first ballet, *Tones*, which she dedicated to her grandmother.

Tania gained so much strength from her family who recognized her talents early on and nurtured them. Opportunities to compose and conduct came from serendipity, but Tania excelled with each new opportunity, bringing her love for music and for the people who create it to every performance and interaction.

In the almost 60 years Tania has spent in New York, she has made remarkable contributions, not only with her music, but also with her work leading artistic organizations. Tania creates change wherever she goes, always supporting other composers along the way whom she calls "the kings and queens of sound," and her passion for music is infectious. Her composition *Stride* won the 2021 Pulitzer Prize and Tania herself became a Kennedy Center Honoree in 2022. Despite such a busy schedule, Tania makes time to encourage young composers to follow their voices with her organization Composers Now, dedicated to empowering all living composers, celebrating the diversity of their voices, and honoring the significance of their artistic contributions to the cultural fabric of society.

NOBUO
UEMATSU

Composer who brings games to life

A composer of video game music was not a profession in the 1980s. With a bit of luck and a lot of creativity, Nobuo Uematsu created a life-long profession writing music for video games. Having no formal music education, Nobuo taught himself the piano after being inspired and enthralled with the music of Elton John. While playing at pubs in a local band, an employee of a gaming company approached him and asked if he would be interested in trying to write for video games. Nobuo agreed and started learning to write within the capabilities of the 1980s gaming system which, at the time, could only produce three unique sounds at whatever pitch the composer desired. So, with a very limited palette, Nobuo got to work and within two years produced the soundtrack to the wildly successful game *Final Fantasy*.

As technology improved, more sounds became available to Nobuo and the complexity of his music expanded until recorded music could accompany the games. His music elevated the games it accompanied, evolving over time to blur the lines between video game music, popular music, and concert music. His 1997 theme for *Final Fantasy VII*, "One Winged Angel," incorporated vocals, a trend that would continue across the video game world thereafter. Nobuo has written music for over 80 games including for the *Final Fantasy* franchise for over three decades. Nobuo's music became so popular that it took to the concert stage as orchestras around the world perform to sold out concerts for fans of his music. Despite his success, Nobuo remains humble, accessible, and always smiling, just as happy to discuss music or his other passions, cycling and professional wrestling, over a beer.

NOBUO UEMATSU

Born 1959
KOCHI (JAPAN)

ICONIC
COMPOSERS

DAVID LEE
CSICSKO

is an award-winning artist and designer whose distinctive artwork, stained glass, and mosaics beautify train stations, hospitals, and universities across the Midwest and East Coast. His many credits include designing the Obamas' White House Christmas in 2012. David's lively illustrations can also be seen in *The Skin You Live In* from the Chicago Children's Museum, now in its 16th printing, *LGBTQ+ Icons*, and *Science People*, the first two books of the People Series. Through his use of color, bold graphics and playful patterns, David Lee Csicsko celebrates the richness and diversity of life.

NICHOLAS
CSICSKO

is fascinated by the connection between music, economics, and the world. After receiving a Doctorate of Music in composition from The Juilliard School, Nicholas has gone on to become an institutional investor, managing the endowments of non-profit organizations while lecturing and writing on music.

EMI
FERGUSON

collaborates with living composers to help shape the future of music in addition to invigorating historical music as a flute player, singer, and composer. Growing up between Japan, England, France, and the United States, Emi came to New York City to study at The Juilliard School and brings her love of music and performing to audiences around the globe.

© 2023 Trope Industries LLC.

This book and any portion thereof may not be reproduced or used in any manner whatsoever without the express written permission of the publisher. All rights reserved.

© 2023 Illustrations by David Lee Csicsko
© 2023 Text by Nicholas Csicsko & Emi Ferguson
LCCN: 2022951415
ISBN: 978-1-9519631-4-9

Printed and bound in China
First printing, 2023

David Lee Csicsko's illustrations from
Iconic Composers are available for purchase.
For inquiries, go to trope.com or email
the gallery at info@trope.com.

+ INFORMATION:
For additional information
on our books and prints,
visit trope.com

For additional resources
on all things music, visit
trope.com/iconiccomposers

2 1982 32413 5684